The Inner-Beauty Secret

Writt

© 2015 by YouthLight, Inc.
Chapin, SC 29036

Project Layout by Amy Rule

Project Editing by Susan Bowman

All rights reserved. No part of this book may be reproduced or transmitted in any form or by any means, electronic, mechanical, including photocopying, recording, or by any information storage and retrieval system, except in the case of reviews, without the express written permission of the publisher, except where permitted by law.

ISBN: 978-1-59850-163-6

Library of Congress Control Number: 2014946787

10 9 8 7 6 5 4 3 2 1
Printed in the United States of America

Illustrated By: Kathy Voerg

This book is dedicated to my loving mother, Patricia Howard-Thomas, who taught me that true beauty starts from the inside and shines its way out.

Shhh...

This book is for a secret group.
A group of kids who
are in the loop.

These
kids know
something
that others don't.
They know a secret
that some won't.

This secret is as old as it can be.
It has been around since the date was B.C.

It's a secret you can search for...

FAR and **wide.**

But, this secret is really found **inside.**

Knowing this secret makes the world a greater place.
Shhh... This secret has nothing to do with your face.

It does not involve your body or the clothes that you wear.

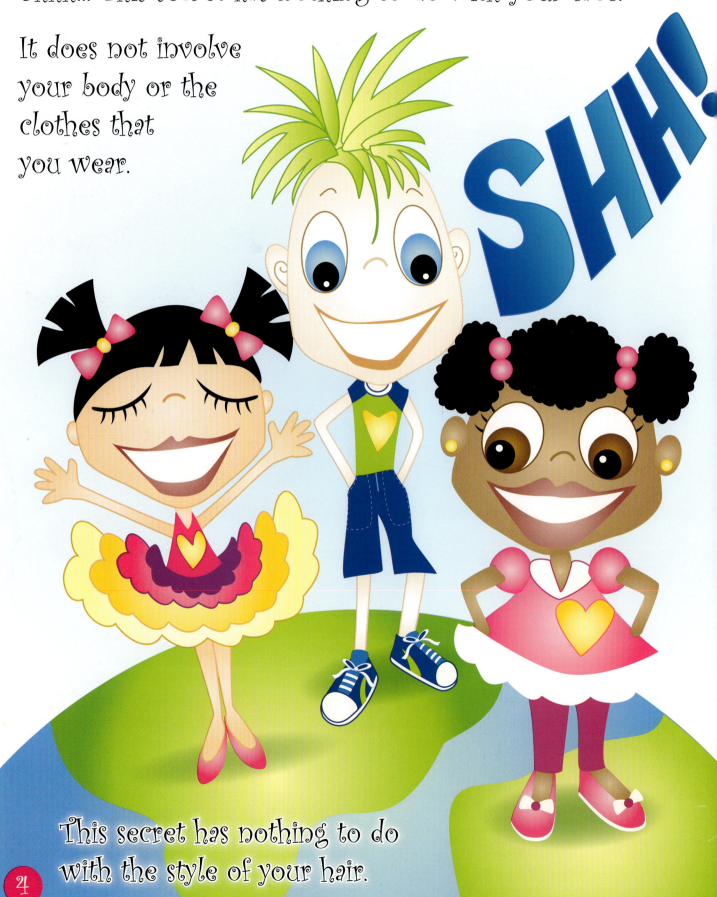

This secret has nothing to do with the style of your hair.

Your eyes can be BLUE, Green, or BROWN. Your teeth can be straight or twisted around. You could be thin, wide, or in between. You could be short and round, or tall and lean.

Come in closer...
I will tell you now.

If you want to be beautiful
I'll show you how...

SHHH

Inner-beauty is the secret inside of you.

It lives in your heart, and tells you what to do.

Inner-beauty is not in the shape of your body nor in the style of your hair, when you are beautiful; your actions show

kindness and care.

Your attitude can be good or bad. Your behavior in school can make your teacher happy or sad.

Your inner-beauty is the voice that tells you to do what is right.

It tells you to be your best, even when no one else is in sight.

When bullies try to hurt your friends, your inner-beauty sticks up for them - and it wins.

You report the bullies, and then adults ask them to stop.

Your inner-beauty made the right decision, because it rocks!

Being **beautiful** means being trustworthy and fair.

When you show inner-beauty, you handle things with care.

The secret is out!
Hip Hip Hooray!

Now, you can start using this secret today!

You've got the power; yes you do, because you've already got beauty inside of you!

You say "please," "thank you," and follow the Golden Rule.

Your manners are polite, because your inner-beauty is ridiculously cool!

Being responsible is a sign of true inner-beauty;

you do what you say you'll do, because that's your beautiful duty.

This inner-beauty SPARKLES and SHINES

and unlike outer-beauty, it lasts throughout time.

Inner-Beauty Tips for Parents & Educators

1. Praise children for their positive character traits instead of their appearance. Example: "I noticed that you helped Stacy when she dropped her backpack. You are such a nice friend to her."

2. Encourage children to give back to the community. Community service is a great way to help others while gaining the spirit of compassion. When children volunteer, it can open their eyes to a new way of life. It can also help them appreciate their own.

3. Take advantage of teachable moments. If you and your child/student notice someone (either in person or on television) acting in a way that is not inner-beautiful, take note of that situation and then have a discussion about it. Ask, "What did he/she notice?" and "What could that person have done differently?"

4. Challenge yourself. Try not to engage in "fat talk" or negative talk about your appearance and about other people. The media sends enough negative messages regarding body image to children. Try not to let the messages that they receive from you be negative, as well. Instead, let them see you feeling good about your body, and let them see you compliment others on something not body related. Example: "Did you get a chance to taste Aunt Lauren's lasagna? Wow...she is a great cook!"

5. Model inner-beauty by speaking kind words and doing the right thing in tough situations. Children watch adults to see their actions. Let your actions always reflect inner-beauty by being kind and respectful.

Want to know more?
Check out these resources!

DOWNLOAD FREE FOLLOW-UP WORKSHEETS FOR *THE INNER-BEAUTY SECRET*
www.youthlight.com/wkshts/ibs.pdf

www.Pearl-Girls.org
PEARL Girls is a self-esteem organization for girls. Since 2006, PEARL Girls has been hosting empowering programs that uplift, educate, and motivate!

www.CoachKeisha.com
Keisha Howard, "Coach Keisha" is the author of *The Inner-Beauty Secret*. She firmly believes that "An Empowered woman begins with a Confident girl." Through speaking presentations and Confidence Coaching, Coach Keisha is on a mission to spread her message of self-love, confidence and inner-beauty.

www.self-esteem-nase.org
The National Association for Self-esteem. This website is dedicated to helping every person understand self-esteem and experience personal happiness.

www.dove.us/Social-Mission/campaign-for-real-beauty.aspx
The Dove Campaign for Real Beauty. This site rocks! It's whole purpose is to re-define the definition of beauty. Tons of videos, games, and other resources related to girl's self-esteem can be downloaded.

www.girlsinc.org
A national organization that provides after-school activities based on a curriculum to help girls become smart, strong, and bold.

www.bodypositive.com
A great site dedicated to boosting body image appreciation!

www.kidshealth.org
A great educational tool for kids, parents, and educators. Many topics related to body and health are covered, and the site is divided according to its audience, so it's a great resource for everyone.

www.something-fishy.org
A great resource for information regarding Eating Disorders.

www.hghw.org
An awesome site dedicated to girl empowerment!

www.kidsempowered.com
Kids Empowered offers programs and training to empower children, parents and professionals to deal with unfriendly classmates and friends, bullying, relational aggression and to build confidence, emotional intelligence, self-esteem, fitness and social skills.